KILLER VIRUS Exposed!

New covid strains & the great reset, agenda 2030,
5G chips and vaccine passports?

-

Deep state & the elite - population Control – a
globalist future?

AF417496

Rebel Press Media

Disclaimer

Our other books

Check out our other books for other unreported news, exposed facts and debunked truths, and more.

Join the exclusive Rebel Press Media Circle!

You will get new updates about the unreported reality delivered in your inbox every Friday.

Sign up here today:

https://campsite.bio/rebelpressmedia

Introduction: No Evidence?

National Center for Immunization and Respiratory Disease: SARS-CoV-2 virus never isolated from even one patient - CDC director acknowledges on TV that 'vaccines' do NOT prevent infections

So indeed it was all just the flu or some other existing respiratory virus. That much can now be said with certainty after the CDC finally responded to several WOB requests, acknowledging that no proof can be given of an isolated - and thus objectively proven to exist - virus that would cause Covid-19. So what skeptics have been calling for over a year, and what has been dismissed by politicians and media as "fake news" and "disinformation" ever since, is now the confirmed truth: the corona crisis is, medically speaking, one big hoax. People who ended up in the hospital most likely all had and have influenza and/or pneumonia. Therefore, it has been a purely political decision, under the guise of a "new" respiratory virus, to incrementally destroy the economy and freedom of society to enable the communist "Great Reset" and "Agenda 2030.

Last year we already pointed out several FOIA (= WOB) requests by Canadian investigative journalist Christine Massey and her team. She asked authorities around the world for scientific proof that the SARS-CoV-2 virus was isolated from even one patient, and would demonstrably cause the (supposed) disease 'Covid-19'. (See also our articles of 11-03: € 225,000 reward offered

for providing proof of existence of SARS-CoV-2; 11-04:
'Laboratories in US cannot find Covid-19 in not one of
1500 positive tested'' (/ Tests at 7 universities of ALL
people examined showed that they do not have Covid,
but Influenza A or B) and 20-12-2020: Despite 40 WOB
requests worldwide, not one authority can provide
proof of SARS-CoV-2).

On June 7, there was finally a response (#21-01075-
FOIA) from the CDC: "A search of our files revealed no
documents related to your request. The National Center
for Immunization and Respiratory Disease specifically
informs us that the CDC does not purify or isolate any
Covid-19 virus in the manner described by the
submitter.'

Totally debunked test remains basic European policy

In other words, the CDC has never been able to isolate
the SARS-CoV-2 virus. Scientifically, this removes any
basis for assuming a 'new' virus would cause a 'new'
disease. Recently, the CDC decided to ban the PCR test
as of January 1, 2022, precisely because it cannot
distinguish it from a regular flu, and because the huge
number of false positives makes this test completely
unreliable anyway.

(And yet this totally debunked test also continues to be
abused by European governments for even more
oppressive and discriminatory exclusionary measures
and soon new totalitarian lockdowns.)

Dr. Robert O.Young's website points to other CDC documents that would show that the HPV virus, the measles virus, the MERS virus, the Zika virus and the polio virus, among others, have never been isolated and purified from a patient (the same would apply to the HIV virus). 'The CDC has been making up the science behind global "pandemics" for decades, using the media to create mass hysteria when no pandemic existed,' observes Mike 'Natural News' Adams.

Zika virus hoax

Another recent example is the Zika virus, which we also covered. Mainstream media spread fear by claiming that this 'Zika virus' caused microcephaly (smaller / malformed skulls) in babies. Pharmaceutical companies were given billions to develop a vaccine, but the Zika virus turned out to be nothing more than yet another hype.

In fact, there was clear evidence that the birth defects were actually caused by earlier vaccines, and a "virus" was falsely blamed to ensure that the real culprit was not known to the public.

CDC director acknowledges that vaccines do not prevent 'infections'

The complete corona hoax is falling apart now that CDC Director Dr. Rochelle Walensky has admitted on TV that the 'vaccines' do NOT prevent infections. Whether or not there are infections with viruses and variants that may or may not exist is irrelevant here. What matters is that one of the highest medical bosses in the US is hereby confirming that the Covid-19 'vaccines' are completely useless in medical terms, and the 'test/vaccine passport' is nothing but proof of absolute blind obedience to a political agenda, and not of one's 'immune status'.

'Spike protein injections ('prop pricks') are deadly biological weapons'

'While the Covid-19 virus appears to be nothing more than a relabeled cold virus, the spike protein toxic nanoparticle - now being injected via 'vaccines' - is a deadly biological weapon started in the US, and fortified with US taxpayer money in Wuhan,' Adams writes. 'It now seems clear that the purpose of the Covid hysteria was to get people to accept spike protein (encoding) injections en masse, deliberately falsely labelled as 'vaccines.'

'These spike proteins cause blood clots, which is why the Covid vax is now called the 'clot shot' (the 'clot prick'). (See also our 14-07 article: Canadian doctor tests his vaccinated patients: 62% already have blood clots). They also cause neurological damage, brain hemorrhages, heart attacks, spontaneous abortions and overall blood vessel damage, even according to the mainstream (extremely pro-vaccine) Salk Institute.'

'The spike protein was developed as a bioweapon to cause a range of symptoms falsely called 'Covid', which is then used to push through even more injections of even more (spike) bioweapons. The Covid-19 'virus' is just a cocktail concoction of cold and herpes viruses... The purpose of all this? Depopulation.'

'Every person who cooperates is an accomplice to crimes against humanity'

'The spike protein is a depopulation weapon,' Adams continued. 'The 'vaccine' is a Soylent Green-like extermination/suicide shot packaged as a 'drug. The 'pandemic' was media hysteria intended to cause panic so that people would clamor for a vaccine en masse and not resist these extermination shots. This means that many who received this shot will soon be dead, because the whole point of this fake pandemic is to get rid of billions of people in this world.'

'This also means that every person who participates in this is complicit in genocidal murder and crimes against humanity. That includes journalists, scientists, doctors, politicians, the FDA/CDC/WHO (/RIVM/GGD/EMA) officials, and even local pharmacists and nurses who are poking these kill shots into men, women, children and the elderly. Compared to their crimes against humanity, the Holocaust of WW-2 is child's play. Indeed, during the Covid vaccine Holocaust, billions of people may well be murdered before these criminals are stopped.'

'You are witnessing a mass extermination campaign'

'In essence, you are now witnessing a global mass extermination campaign disguised as a public health response to a pandemic. This is the most sinister and diabolical "science" hoax ever perpetrated in the history of modern civilization. It is, in all honesty, a globalist attempt at homo sapiens extinction, a kind of planetary 'ethnic cleansing' to rid the world of (by far the most) humans, and pave the way for whatever insane scenario they have in mind next.'

'It is time for all human beings who wish to save the human race to peacefully rise up, and oppose this genocidal extermination attempt on humanity.'

Politicians like Senator Rand Paul are therefore urging everyone to simply say NO to new lockdowns, mouthguards, social distancing, testing, Covid passports, and of course the injections. 'They can't arrest all of us. They can't keep all the children out of school... We don't have to accept these harmful measures from these insignificant tyrants and weak bureaucrats. (Say:) 'We will not allow you to harm our children any more this year.'

'Globalists want to remove few billion people'

'We've all been misled, folks,' Adams concludes. 'None of this had anything to do with public health, saving lives or stopping a pandemic. This is a meticulous, coordinated play to get people to commit suicide with bioweapon injections so the globalists can remove a few billion people from this planet, and impose their tyranny and authoritarian control on the survivors.'

'It may also be the cover for their planned financial reset, which will collapse the world currency, destroy all the financial 'assets' of the sheeple, and transfer the ownership of everything into the hands of the globalist elite.'

Whether it will really be as bad as Mike Adams - and by now many others - fears, we do not dare say at this moment. But one thing seems certain: the Covid injections are going to cause an unimaginable public health crisis with unprecedented numbers of victims in Europe alone.

This book is a compilation of our articles published earlier and new articles to expose the vaccines with the fitting context, regarding topics such as depopulation and world control by the globalist elite, if you would like to know more about subjects such as the great reset, we would advise you to read our other books too, and share them with everyone you hold dear.

We want to reach as many people as possible, that's why keep publishing our content, to make sure that if one title gets ignored, the other title still gets the attention, these subjects need.

If we want to win this war against humanity, we have to inform everyone about the reality of what is happening right now!

Please support us by leaving positive reviews on every platform, so we can continue to push the truth out there and make sure to wake up as many people as possible. Freedom through truth and we can only change our future if we have the majority!

Table of Contents

Chapter 1: Vaccine deaths exposed!

Infectious disease specialist: 'This is a global time bomb: eventually ANY vaccinated person will suffer adverse effects'

The lie persisted for months that the Covid-19 vaccinations only remain in muscle tissue has already been definitively debunked in several scientific studies. Now an autopsy on a deceased vaccinated person has shown that the genetic mRNA instructions - like the spike protein produced by the vaccines - do indeed spread throughout the body to all organs. A shocked infectious disease specialist from New Jersey, who did not want to be named for fear of reprisals, responded that "this means that eventually ANY vaccinated person will experience adverse side effects. And because vaccinated people have been turned into permanent 'spike factories' by this mRNA, those effects will most likely be irreversible. 'This is a global time bomb,' is therefore his conclusion.

The autopsy on a Covid-vaccinated man is said to have been the first of its kind, and revealed that in the deceased 86-year-old man, 'viral RNA' was found in virtually all his organs 24 days after his injection.

No Covid, negative test, then ADE caused by fatal vaccine-virus combo

After his first Pfizer shot on January 9, the man developed increasing health problems, requiring hospitalization after 18 days. However, he had no clinical Covid symptoms, and his test was also negative. The post-mortem report therefore states that "no morphological changes due to Covid" were found in his body.

Medical authorities say that the 86-year-old contracted Covid through another patient on the ward, but the autopsy proves that the damage to his organs was done before he was admitted. That actually leaves only one cause: the vaccine. And when the man was indeed infected in the hospital, he didn't stand a chance, and had an ADE (Antibody Dependent Enchancement) reaction, which numerous independent scientists (such as Professor Pierre Capel) and experts have been warning about for months.

Virus RNA created by vaccine mRNA?

'The vaccine could not stop the virus from penetrating every organ,' writes American radio host Hal Turner. However, there is another possible explanation: that 'viral RNA' was in reality created by the vaccine mRNA.

Finally, all vaccines licensed in the West encode the body to produce the spike protein of the (supposed) virus. A recent Pfizer study in Japan showed that only this spike protein - intentionally modified to better bind to human ACE2 receptors - is responsible for all health damage, and spreads throughout the body after vaccination, including to the brain, as also shown in a recent Nature Neuroscience study.

In summary, the logical inference is:

** if the body is full of 'viral RNA', which would have caused the patient to die*

** and it is established that only the spike protein is the dangerous part of the virus*

** and the mRNA vaccines instruct the human body to make just that spike protein*

** in such a way that it adheres to human cells even better than the viral spike protein.*

** then the patient has died as a result of an ADE caused by that spike protein*

** which must have come (mainly) from the vaccine, because he had no Covid-19 when he was admitted with health problems 18 days after his vaccination.*

People who still tell others and themselves that they were 'vaccinated months ago and have nothing to worry about' should also consider that the consequences of these deliberate DNA changes can be compared to cancer: it can develop very quickly, but also very slowly. Only, once it is there, it never goes away by itself.

Are vaccines already affecting judgment?

'Have to think,' we just wrote. But can some vaccinated people still do that? We received a message from a contact who wrote that he had tried desperately to keep two of his friends off the vaccine. To no avail. Both friends got vaccinated anyway; one is now constantly suffering from his heart racing, the other had to be hospitalized with severe thrombosis (anonymized info published with permission).

And you guessed it: doctors involved declared even before diagnosis and examination that it could not possibly be due to the vaccine. And the victims bizarrely believed this too. It is, of course, speculation, but is this inability to think logically, to make good judgments, to draw conclusions, perhaps the result of brain damage caused by those same vaccines?

'Global time bomb'

An infectious disease specialist in New Jersey said he was enormously shocked when he read the autopsy report. 'People think that only a minority suffer side effects from the vaccine. Based on this study, it means that eventually everyone will get side effects, because these spike proteins bind to ACE2 receptors all over your body.'

16

'That mRNA should have stayed at the injection site, but it doesn't. That means that the spike proteins made by the mRNA will also get into every organ. And we know that it is this spike protein that does the damage.'

Chapter 2: China working with the US?

Why did China NOT use the challenged mRNA/DNA technology in its own vaccines? - NIH director: 'SARS-1 and MERS also come from there'

And yet another 'conspiracy theory' that turns out to be a hard fact, thereby exposing yet another lie perpetuated for months by the mainstream media and politicians. Dr. Francis Collins, the current director of the American National Institutes of Health (NIH), has frankly admitted in an interview that the Americans and the Chinese collaborated to make the coronavirus more contagious to humans ('gain of function') in the biohazard-4 lab in Wuhan. Dr. Anthony Fauci, who is in ever greater trouble because of his many lies that have now been proven, denied to the Senate in March that he and his colleague Collins had funded the "gain of function" research in the Wuhan lab. Now he appears to have committed perjury about that.

'SARS and MERS come from there'

Collins' statements are also highly incriminating for Dr. Peter Daszak, who through his Ecohealth Alliance received substantial grants from the NIH to fund the 'gain of function' research in Wuhan. Collins explained in detail how the NIH and the Wuhan Institute of Virology work together. He insisted that there is 'good reason' for this, as both SARS-1 and MERS 'originated there'.

Mike 'Natural News' Adams hears in this that both SARS and MERS come from the Wuhan laboratory, but in my opinion by 'there' Collins meant China in general. Indeed, SARS-1 first surfaced in China in 2003. Its spread was subsequently limited to four other countries.

However, MERS was first detected in Saudi Arabia in 2012 (see also our article yesterday: Medical journals announce potential new pandemic: MERS-CoV). Adams is therefore right to wonder, after all, if "Collins has more information that these relatively new and deadly coronaviruses (SARS, MERS) both came from the Wuhan lab?

Conspiracy theory turns out to be hard fact

Dr. Collins, Daszak and Fauci worked directly with the infamous 'bat lady' Dr. Shi Zhengli, who is funded and rewarded by the Chinese Communist Party (CCP), according to press reports from the Wuhan lab. The Wuhan Institute of Virology is also the center of a 'United Front Group' established to neutralize all potential opposition and criticism of the CCP. When the lab was identified as a possible source of the coronavirus last year, China blocked a WHO investigation into it. Then, for months, Dr. Fauci proclaimed the now-proven crystal-clear lies, and even committed perjury about it.

The same applies to Dr. Daszak, regularly quoted in Western media, who kept insisting that an artificial origin of the virus, i.e. a "lab leak" - intentional or otherwise - was a "conspiracy theory". Scientists who pointed out the many inconsistencies and factual evidence that the bat soup or seafood market theory, also accepted as 'true' in Europe, is pure nonsense, were virulently attacked and blackened. This even happened to HIV-discoverer and Nobel Prize winner Luc Montagnier.

Walking 'COVID factories'

Fauci, Daszak and other system scientists have also gone all out to inject the entire world population with experimental genetic manipulation "vaccines," which have now been shown to turn people into walking "spike factories" that are also "shed" (exhaled) into the environment. In previous articles we pointed out the growing number of scientific studies and reports that those exhaled 'spikes' can also cause damage to the health of unvaccinated people.

If that is placed in the light of the leaked 'Fauci Files', from which it emerged that the coronavirus was already referred to internally as a deliberately created 'bioweapon' on March 11, 2020, then a terrifying picture emerges that is probably too much for most people to take in all at once.

Chinese vaccines contain no mRNA - why not there, and here?

Consider the following: soon after the outbreak of the corona pandemic, China shared all the information about the (supposed) SARS-CoV-2 virus with the world, including the complete genetic construction plan. Based on this, new vaccines based on mRNA and DNA technology, never used or tested on humans, were developed in America, Europe, Russia and India, with which the largest medical experiment in history is now being conducted by injecting as many people and even children as possible with it.

However, the Chinese vaccines do not contain this mRNA/DNA technology. There, the society and economy have been running normally for quite some time. What could be the reason that the Chinese did not want to inject mRNA instructions into their population? Were they perhaps fully aware of the gigantic risks that would entail?

An even more important question: why was and is it done here?

21

Chapter 3: Facebook bought by big pharma?

Judicial Watch provides evidence after WOB request of close cooperation between Facebook, the CDC and the Bill & Melinda Gates Foundation in manipulating coverage of the corona pandemic - Ministry of Truth has completely displaced real journalism in the West to alternative channels

No matter how reliable your sources have usually proven to be, sometimes you do make an error of judgment based on convincing information, as happened yesterday with the article about an alleged concentration camp in Canada, which turned out to be a facility for workers working on a new gas pipeline. (Our great thanks to some readers who pointed this out to us. Active reading and thinking along, and correcting it if necessary, is much appreciated!) Of course, mainstream media 'fact checkers' immediately jump on these kinds of partly incorrect reports, but how reliable are they themselves when it is considered that for example the well-known Factcheck.org (Facebook) is financed by the parent company of vaccine manufacturer Johnson & Johnson?

U.S. Congressman Thomas Massie recently pointed this out in several tweets when Facebook had once again removed so-called "misinformation" about vaccines. The Factcheck.org used by Facebook is in fact funded by the Robert Wood Johnson Foundation, whose CEO

Richard Besser is not entirely coincidentally a former director of the CDC. The foundation holds more than $1.8 billion in Johnson & Johnson stock, one of the four major Covid-19 vaccine manufacturers.

Ministry of Truth has supplanted real journalism

This is downright deceitful, because did you really think that Facebook's "fact checker" would post or confirm any negative reports about the products of its largest funder? Of course, not - factcheck.org is - just like the other big media fact checkers - a propaganda tool of the pharmaceutical industry, Big Tech and globalist system politics.

Official 'fact checkers' have become a core part of the Orwellian 'Ministry of Truth' that in the West has completely displaced once independent journalism into alternative channels.

Certainly in Europe, almost ALL reports in the mainstream media on important topics such as health, vaccines, climate, energy, immigration, science and society are politicized and framed, meant to give you a perception of a prescribed reality that has little or nothing to do with the truth anymore.

Facebook / CDC / Bill Gates collaborate closely on corona narrative

More news about Facebook (/ 'Fakebook'): the well-known 'watchdog' Judicial Watch has published evidence obtained via a WOB request (2469 documents, including official emails) showing that Facebook works closely with the CDC in controlling and manipulating the reporting of the corona p(l)andemic. Facebook also provided the CDC with $3 million worth of free advertising space.

For example, on January 26, 2020, just days after a senior official from the Bill & Melinda Gates Foundation put the CDC in touch with Facebook, the social media giant informed the CDC what actions would be taken to combat "misinformation" about the Chinese Communist Party (CCP) and the "Wuhan" virus. Under the title "FB coronavirus narrative," Facebook said it was working with more than "60 fact-checking organizations" that review posts in more than 50 languages for their content.

We have emphasized the word 'narrative' because it again underscores the fact that it was decided from the outset that only one predetermined desired version of the outbreak of this supposed virus should appear in the media. Corona was then still mainly limited to China, but all over the world media and fact checkers were prepared and instructed to manipulate the population to adopt only this official version.

Bill Gates is also the biggest sponsor of the "fact checker" Politifact, which is used by Facebook and

Google to spread disinformation about the Covid-19 gene therapy injections, such as that these would be "vaccines" that would be "proven safe.

'Facebook might not exist after 2035'

So Mark Zuckerberg lied flat out when he claimed that Facebook is 'not the government. American economist Martin Armstrong believes that Facebook 'has now lost all immunity, and can be sued directly for violating everyone's civil rights.'

'Has Zuckerberg thus demonstrated that he is not qualified to run a company of this size? The increased share prices have nothing to do with his management skills.' Although Facebook's own statistics show otherwise, the inevitable decline does not appear to be long in coming. Armstrong: 'He may think he's a demigod and omnipotent, but sometimes the higher they are, the deeper they fall. Facebook might not exist after 2035.'

Chapter 4: Corruption and manipulation?

'Google, Facebook and other Big Tech manipulate humanity like never before in history' - Proven fact-checkers mainstream media predominantly tell lies

On August 18, the already high-profile documentary 'Plandemic II: inDOCTORnation' was released. In the free-to-view film, one fact after another is presented about the manipulation and corruption of the mainstream and social media, Bill Gates, the vaccine industry, and the well-known corona 'experts' used by governments to instill fear in the population. This documentary also concludes that the global corona pandemic hoax is a purposeful agenda to bring all of humanity under total control, while simultaneously lavishing Big Pharma with billions of taxpayer dollars.

'This is a must-see documentary that will absolutely make you fall off your chair, and forever change your understanding of the total corruption of the 'scientific' establishment, and the for-profit medical system,' comments Mike 'Natural News' Adams. 'In essence, there has been a group of evil people who have created this virus and unleashed it on the world so they can crush humanity and make billions in profits. Even more shocking is that this is not the first time they have tried this.'

'Google, Facebook and other Big Tech manipulate humanity like never before in history'

'Search engines (like Google) are the holy grail for those who want control over the narrative (=what people are told),' begins one of the shorter clips from the docu, uploaded to make the information more accessible to the many people with shorter attention spans. 'Google is already more powerful in controlling people's lives than almost any government in the world.'

At a U.S. Congressional hearing, a psychologist testified that Google, Facebook and Twitter and other 'Big Tech' companies are able to manipulate 15 million voters into voting or not voting for a particular candidate or party in the U.S. alone. 'And the methods they use are invisible,' Dr. Robert Epstein explained. 'They're subliminal, and more powerful than any other method I've encountered during my 40-year career in behavioral sciences.'

Zach Vorhies, Google engineer and whistleblower, pointed out that Google has stated under oath that it does not maintain a 'blacklist', but that this was a lie, because the list does exist. 'As an engineer, I investigated Google's internal search engine. I discovered that they have blacklisted numerous search terms, such as 'cancer cure' and 'cure cancer'. Why does Google decide what people can or cannot search for?'

Fact-checkers mainstream media preaching mostly lies

Google has changed from the best search engine to "a network for global control, data collection, and social engineering ," the docu continues. The same goes for the so-called 'fact-checkers'. The globally known Snopes was founded in 1995 by a couple who had no journalistic training, background or experience whatsoever. Google is Snopes' main source for 'checking' whether something is 'true' or 'false'.

Time and again, however, Snopes itself turns out to be a source of lies. For example, it was claimed that it was not true that Dr. Judy Mikovits (to whom we also devoted an extensive article on this site on May 10) had been arrested without a warrant and without charges because of her critical scientific opinion about vaccines, and in particular the upcoming Covid-19 vaccines. Snopes only needed to request the official arrest documents, or consult Dr. Mikovits lawyers, to see that it was indeed the truth.

Facebook's Politifact, which has a direct "hotline" with the WHO, is at least as manipulative. The owner of Politifact is the Poynter Institute, which has received large sums of money from Google and the Bill & Melinda Gates Foundation. Politifact and FactCheck.org claimed that it is 'a conspiracy theory' that patents for the coronavirus and treatments for it have been around for years. 'However, they reviewed only 3 of the 4452 publicly viewable patents, which undeniably show that the Sars coronavirus, its detection and treatment, are widely patented in both the public and private sectors.'

Newsreaders, current affairs programs, talk shows 'in service of the same propaganda machine'

'An entire industry is paid to attack and defame journalists and whistleblowers, and ruin their reputations,' the docu continues. Newsreaders and current affairs program headliners 'are not the only highly paid actors employed by the propaganda machine. Most talk shows are owned by the same 'overlords' and follow the same script, but with an added quip.'

In the Netherlands, too, it is a daily tactic to dismiss critics of official policy on corona, the climate, immigration, the EU, et cetera, as 'conspiracy theorists', always citing the most extreme fringe groups (flat earth / flat earth, crop circles, reptilians, etc.). Via 'controlled opposition' websites, too, all serious criticism is cunningly pushed into one absurd 'alu hat' or 'geeky' corner, with the intention that the average citizen will no longer even listen to other voices that are serious and substantiated.

'This is mass hysteria!'

The docu repeats an oft-quoted excerpt from the film 'Network' (1976). In it, a famous TV presenter suddenly rants to the audience in the studio: 'Television is not the truth! We have only created illusions, there is NOTHING true about it! But you, people of all ages, colors and species, sit and watch us day after day, night after night,

and you begin to believe the illusions we are telling you.
You are beginning to believe that TV is reality, and your
own lives are unreal.'

'This is mass hysteria, you maniacs! You are real, and we
are the illusion! So turn off your televisions NOW, and
leave them off!

A call that 44 years many should take to heart. The only
way that the scales can fall from your eyes, with which
your deprogramming can begin, is indeed by
immediately stopping watching and listening to the
well-known 'news' and 'current affairs' programs, with
their adulated leaders, who are mere perception
managers for an elite that for years has been working
hard to take away everything we hold dear, all our
freedoms, and our entire lives and futures. The Covid-
19 pandemic hoax is the sad culmination of this
unprecedented mass hysteria fuelled by media and
politics.

Plandemic II also goes into detail about the real
background and motives of Bill Gates, the oft-discussed
Event-201 (around the corona pandemic already
planned for 2019), and the criminal fraud and
corruption of the vaccine industry. Due to the length of
this article, it would be better to discuss that in possible
separate articles. Moreover, many issues have been
discussed many times on this site as well.

Chapter 5: Vaccine lies?

'People who claim these so-called vaccines are safe are jerks' - Graphene oxide in Pfizer vaccine or not? Fact-checker DPA comes up with nothing better than 'if it's not in the package insert, it's not in there'

Dr. Michael Yeadon, former vice president and chief scientist at Pfizer, has given several interviews this year about the Covid-19 'vaccines'. Despite his knowledge and career, he is now being dismissed by 'fact checkers' as an 'anti-vaxxer' and conspiracy theorist who would make 'unsubstantiated statements'. For example, Yeadon says that most of what is being claimed by the media and politicians about the 'vaccines' is nothing but pseudoscientific nonsense, and these injections could actually pose an existential threat to all of humanity. Fact checkers, according to him, tell mere lies. This is certainly true of DPA Factchecking, which recently came out with a similarly inane and misleading "rebuttal" to the Spanish study that discovered graphene oxide in the Pfizer vaccine: "If it's not in the package insert, it's not in it.

Indeed, the media's blind faith and trust in Big Pharma, which has already had to pay millions in damages over the years for causing many thousands of sick and disabled people to die, and for providing faulty and misleading information about the so-called 'safety' of their 'vaccines', is apparently so great that the main reason critical reports and studies are labeled as 'untrue' or 'false' is 'because it's not in the package insert'.

Graphene oxide

This is literally how it is stated in DPA's 'fact checking' following reports that Spanish scientists have found graphene oxide in the Pfizer vaccine (see our article of 05-07: Spanish university scientists discover graphene oxide nanoparticles in Pfizer vaccine). Since graphene oxide has now also been found in a sample of the AstraZeneca vaccine, honest scientists and journalists should at least demand further investigation into this, especially since the use of graphene oxide in vaccines and drugs has been seriously investigated for years. A combination of PEG mRNA layered with graphene oxide could technologically already be used in vaccines.

Graphene oxide, which is mainly used in CO_2 filters and electronics such as cell phones, 5G transmitters and solar panels, is far from being considered safe for mass use in medical and other human products due to its toxicity. Graphene is also used to filter viruses, bacteria and chemicals from liquids, and was found in Canada earlier this year in the famous blue mouthguards. These specimens were immediately banned from schools due to the demonstrated danger of inhalation and consequent lung damage. As many as 31.1 million of these mouthguards had been distributed in the meantime.

If there are even suspicions that food products in supermarkets may have been contaminated with a certain substance that can cause allergic reactions, for example (and which are also not listed on the label), then as a precautionary measure those products are immediately withdrawn from the market, and consumers are urged not to use them and to return them to the store. So why isn't this being done with these vaccines? After all, it was a scientific team at the University of Almeria that discovered the graphene oxide in a Pfizer vaccine. Why didn't the government do many more spot checks right after that?

And when was the last time you bought fruit or vegetables with a sticker on them containing ingredients such as the special edible coatings used to keep the products fresh for longer and/or to preserve their color? In short, far from all ingredients need to be disclosed to consumers. We learned from a good contact a few years ago that the packaged carrots you buy in the supermarket are so sweet because they are "injected" (/coated) with a special sweetener that does NOT need to be disclosed on the packaging.

Fact-checking Reuters 'laughable gibberish'

News agency Reuters claimed in a "fact checking" article that Dr. Yeadon used "a mix of straw men and fabrication" when he said that asymptomatic spread is a lie, and that the concept of variants used is "idiotic. Indeed, it was always undisputed in science that there is no such thing as asymptomatic infections - until 2020 dawned, and all prevailing scientific principles, including natural group immunity, were suddenly thrown in the trash, and replaced with nonsense reasoning bordering on insanity, not to mention outright lie propaganda.

Yeadon's response: 'There is a fantastic peer-reviewed paper showing that domestic infection in asymptomatic cases was actually ZERO. And I can show several good papers showing that T-cells in convalescent or immunocompromised cases recognize ALL previously known variants, as could be expected based on the fundamentals of immunology. The drivel in their paper about antibodies is laughable.'

People who call these vaccines safe are 'jerks'

Once again, the former Pfizer chief executive and scientific officer does not hide his anger at what is happening. People who claim that these so-called vaccines are "safe" he literally calls "jerks. Indeed, even the official Western figures (VAERS, Yellow Card and EMA) show that these injections are causing a true slaughter unparalleled in medical history. The EMA could have known this, but ignored all the open calls and warnings from scientists that these 'vaccines' are going to cause blood clots in most people, and therefore should be withdrawn immediately.

Injecting pregnant women finds Yeadon even more appalling. 'Nobody in their right mind gives experimental treatments to pregnant women. That is reckless, especially since the reproductive tests are incomplete.' Indeed, these were not completed last year for these injections, as Pfizer's package insert also stated. Recently, shocking figures emerged: as many as 82% of a large group of vaccinated pregnant women had suffered a spontaneous abortion after vaccination.

Tests were recently done with mice, though. The researchers discovered 'a particularly disturbing concentration' of vaccine substances in the ovaries. 'A very recent paper was shown that within days of vaccination, young women produce antibodies to syncytin-1,' a protein that is crucial for a pregnancy to succeed.

In December 2020, Yeadon and other scientists submitted another petition to the EMA, pointing out the cross-reactivity between the spike protein and human syncytin-1. With current events confirming this, the risk of mass infertility in vaccinated women and girls should be front page news everywhere.

'Politicians should be prosecuted for crimes against humanity'

Yeadon calls the entire vaccination campaign a "hoax. The number of vaccine deaths in the US and EU recently stood at around 27,000, and the number of people with serious (often permanent) health damage is already in the many hundreds of thousands. Where are the popular protests against this? Where are the parliamentarians asking critical questions about this by far largest medical scandal of all time?

Politicians and institutions that are now imposing these vaccines with increasing force "should all be locked up in a high-security institution," continues Yeadon. In Great Britain alone, in his view, a dozen or so public figures could be arrested immediately and prosecuted as criminals.

Because in most countries the same thing is happening as in Great Britain - and sometimes worse - 'this scourge is a deception of unprecedented proportions, and crimes against humanity are being committed on a gigantic scale,' the former Pfizer VP believes. In June, he accused the governments and their advisers who pushed these vaccines through of "mass murder.

Chapter 6: Vaccine infections?

Pfizer acknowledges 'shedding' potentially dangerous vaccine-infused substances from person to person via breath and skin contact

A study by the largest Covid-19 'vaccine' manufacturer Pfizer warns that vaccinated people can transmit certain 'vaccine' components to others just by having personal contact with them. Pregnant women and their unborn or newborn child are therefore at risk. Again, this shows that the 'shedding' of potentially harmful 'vaccine' substances such as spike proteins, which we have covered many times this year, is definitely not a conspiracy theory.

'Exposure to the study intervention during pregnancy or lactation and occupational exposure must be reported to Pfizer Safety within 24 hours of disclosure to the investigator,' the document on the clinical study conducted states.

'Study intervention' refers to the mRNA Covid injection. After all, that's what the study is focused on. Exposure' does not mean injection / 'vaccination', but that someone who has NOT been injected comes physically close to someone who has been injected. Additionally, it can also refer to a non-injected person touching the liquid from a vaccine bottle.

Hazard to pregnant and breastfeeding women, and their babies

In this particular study, this refers to non-injected pregnant or breastfeeding women, for example, a worker at a lab or testing facility where the Covid injections are administered. If THAT happens, Pfizer calls it a "safety situation," a safety incident that must be reported within 24 hours.

In short: a lab employee who is pregnant or breastfeeding and gets close to a vaccinated person should report it as soon as possible. Why? Clearly because there is a danger to her unborn child or her newborn baby, to whom that danger may be passed on through breast milk.

So such a woman only needs to get close to someone who has already received the "vaccine. Nothing more. This means that there can be a transfer of 'vaccine' components from one person to another, which Pfizer acknowledges can be a DANGER to pregnant and breastfeeding women and their babies.

From the document, "An EDP (Exposure to the vaccine During Pregnancy) occurs when a male participant who is receiving or has discontinued the study intervention exposes a female partner prior to or during the time of conception. (bold added)

Thus, a vaccinated man getting physically close to his unvaccinated partner - and that doesn't even have to be sex - also presents a dangerous situation for the woman who is going to have a child, wants to have a child, or has just had a child, and for the child itself. Thus, there is a danger of serious damage, disease, or miscarriage just by transferring "vaccine" particles from an injected person to an uninjected person.

Contamination after inhalation or skin contact

The Pfizer document provides an example of a hazardous situation that should be reported immediately: 'A female family member or caregiver reports that she is pregnant after being exposed to the study intervention through inhalation or skin contact...'

'Close contact' therefore includes inhalation of exhaled 'vaccine' substances. You can also become infected with those by simple touch. And no, that doesn't just apply to people who work in labs, test lines or hospitals. Pfizer is talking in general about PEOPLE, one of whom has been vaccinated and the other has not, and about the transfer of 'vaccine' particles from one person to another.

Whether you call that "transferring," "shedding," or "infecting" doesn't matter. Pfizer warns for a reason that such a situation must be reported to the safety department within 24 hours. So the company knew in advance that their product could cause damage to women who are pregnant, who want to become pregnant, who are breastfeeding, AND to the -unborn or born- children themselves. Governments were also aware of this danger; see for example our article of June 8: Germany restricts fundamental right to physical integrity and approves exhalation of spike proteins by vaccinated persons ** (/ (/ 'Shedding' spike proteins by vaccinated persons was already known by German authorities last year, but was kept hidden from the public).

*(** For the record, spike proteins are not IN the injections, but are produced in the body BY the injections).*

Someone could still argue that a pregnant woman may have had contact with a vaccinated person during vaccination where some droplets from the needle may have fallen onto his (or her) skin. However, this is highly unlikely. Pfizer does not mention a time period in the document, but merely outlines the scenario that the man A) was vaccinated, and B) had close contact with a female partner at some point. That could have been days or even weeks later. Any spilled droplets would have been long gone by then.

82% spontaneous abortions after Pfizer injection

The package insert and care instructions discussed extensively on this site stated unequivocally that the Pfizer vaccine should NOT be given to pregnant women, to women who intend to become pregnant within a short period of time, and to women who are breastfeeding. However, this was done from the outset worldwide, in part because Pfizer rescinded the initial warnings for reasons that were unclear.

The consequences of this were recently seen in another scientific study: as many as 82% of 127 women studied who were in their first 20 weeks of pregnancy and who had nevertheless been injected, had a spontaneous abortion.

Biological weapons attack on survival of humanity?

The above does not only apply to the Pfizer vaccine; a few months ago the co-founder of Moderna and also co-developer of the mRNA technology acknowledged that vaccinated people can indeed "shed" vaccine substances such as the Spike protein to their environment.

Despite these shocking facts, almost all politicians worldwide are forcing these injections on their populations with ever more coercive measures, and want to give even more of them, including to ever younger children.

The indications are mounting that we may indeed be facing a direct biological weapons attack on the survival of mankind. An attack, which has actually been openly announced by globalists such as the Rockefellers, Ted

Turner and Bill Gates, who have never made a secret of the fact that they believe there are far too many people walking around on this planet, and something needs to be actively done to "remove" the vast majority.

Chapter 7: No escape?

Member of Canadian government unveiled global roadmap to totalitarian communism in October 2020 in which no one owns anything and everyone must be compulsorily vaccinated!

Yet another country confirming a particularly worrying trend: after the start of the Covid-19 vaccination campaign, the number of sick and dead explodes in Taiwan. The same thing happened before in India, Chile and Seychelles, among others, where more (AstraZeneca) shots were handed out than people live, after which there were 146 times more deaths in 4 months than from corona last year. And as we have been predicting for so long, the authorities refuse to point to the vaccines as the cause, no matter how obvious the statistical link. But the "vaccines" - excuse: experimental genetic gene therapy/manipulation - are now declared untouchable and sacrosanct, and so it is indeed claimed that it is due to a mutation.

Taiwan was rid of corona early this year. Hardly anyone died from Covid-19 anymore, there were hardly any sick people, and life returned to normal - except for the wretched mouth masks, which still had to be worn in public places. The reason for this can only be guessed at, as there was no medical one.

Despite the fact that the umpteenth respiratory virus was under control, the government still began a

43

massive vaccination campaign. This got off to a very slow start in mid-March, but starting in May, the number of people getting injected with experimental mRNA/DNA manipulation suddenly skyrocketed.

EXACTLY at that moment the number of 'cases' and deaths also skyrocketed.

Member of Canadian government revealed road map to totalitarian communism in October

American radio host Hal Turner cites an October 2020 open letter from a member of the Canadian government, which we also published at the time. Here again the most important parts from it:

'I want to give you very important information. I am a committee member of the Liberal Party of Canada. I sit on various committee groups, but the information I give comes from the Strategic Plan Committee (which is controlled by the PMO).' That is the office of left-liberal Prime Minister Justin Trudeau, whose parliament has now given itself unlimited power and an unlimited term without an election as long as there is still a 'pandemic'. Trudeau has thus become Canada's de facto first dictator.

'They have made it very clear that nothing can stop their planned outcome. The roadmap and objectives were drawn up by the prime minister, and go as follows:' (planned time period: late 2020 - late 2021)

44

* 'Introduce second lockdown restrictions gradually. Start with major urban areas first, and then expand;

* Obtain or build isolation facilities in each province at a rapid pace;

* Rapidly increase the number of new 'Covid cases' and 'Covid deaths' so that there is no longer sufficient testing capacity;

* Complete and total second lockdown in 2021, which is much more severe than the first in spring 2020;

* Present the PLANNED Covid-19 mutation or 'reinfection' with a second virus (possibly called Covid-21 (or perhaps SARS-3 or MERS-CoV)), leading to a THIRD wave with a much higher mortality rate and even higher infection rate;

* The health care system is flooded with Covid-19 / Covid-21 patients;

* THIRD lockdown with even stricter measures, such as a complete stop on ALL travel (second/third quarter 2021);

* Implement universal basic income (for the tens of millions of new unemployed who will lose their jobs permanently as a result of this policy. This UBI will be

completely digital, only allowing you to stay alive and watch TV);

* Supply lines collapse, major shortages (stores, supermarkets, online, etc.), major economic instability, followed by chaos, panic, and total dislocation;

* Deploy the military, and establish checkpoints on all major roads. Travel permanently extremely restricted (only by pass / permission). (Third / fourth quarter 2021).'

Depending on the geopolitical situation, the timeline could still change (e.g., 2021 could also be 2022 or 2023), but 'we have been told that in order to initiate this actual economic collapse on an international scale, the federal government is going to offer Canadians a total debt cancellation.' But that comes at a very high price: anyone who claims it gives up forever all rights to all forms of property, and commits to taking all vaccinations offered.

Refusers will initially have to live under very strict lockdown restrictions indefinitely, and thus stay home permanently. But that will only last for a short period, because once the majority of citizens have made the "transition" (to permanent slavery under a global totalitarian communist and transhumanist control system), "the refusers will be characterized as a threat to public safety, and moved to isolation facilities. **Or, in other words, to concentration camps.**

There they will be given one last chance to still
'participate' in the program and have all vaccinations
injected into them. If not, they will remain locked up
permanently and lose all their possessions and rights.
'In the end, the Prime Minister implied that this whole
agenda will be pushed through, regardless of whether
we agree with it or not. And this is not just happening in
Canada. All countries will have similar roadmaps and
agendas. They want to take advantage of the situation
to make large-scale changes' (a financial reset with IMF
world currency, the 'Great Reset', 'Build Back Better',
UN Agenda 2030, the 'Green New Deal').

After the purposefully initiated economic collapse,
many of the tens of millions of unemployed system
followers will be eager for a BOA-Sturmabteilung brown
shirt job in the government, after which they will
impose the above scenario on unwilling fellow citizens
with ruthless cruelty. Friends, neighbors, colleagues,
family and relatives, students and schoolchildren will
betray each other "for the greater good," and will be
happy that the "threats to their health" will be cleared
away for good. (See also: This is how Reichsmarschall
Göring got the people to say, "Scare them and tell them
that refusers are a danger") and Corona policy tears
families and friends apart, exactly as was done in GDR).

Precisely because most people still refuse to believe
that this can and will never happen again, that we are
more civilized nowadays and will never again commit

47

such atrocities, it threatens to happen again. The only thing that can stop this whole process, this preconceived perfidious plan, is a massive awareness, followed by a massive (but we repeat: definitely non-violent!) NO.

Why do politicians want 100% vaccinations? Because then there is no control group left to prove that the oncoming wave of ADEs, blood clots/immune diseases, infertility and deaths is caused by these injections?

Why do politicians want 100% vaccinations? Because then there is no control group left to prove that the oncoming wave of ADEs, blood clots/immune diseases, infertility and deaths is caused by these injections?

The "not being able to buy or sell" foretold in the Bible without the prick of "the Beast" is getting closer and closer as leaders of the globalist propaganda channel CNN openly advocate the exclusion of the unvaccinated from the entire society, and even want to deny them access to supermarkets. In the Philippines, President Duterte has now decided to do this. The vaccine is not mandatory, but if you don't take it, you can literally wither away and starve to death.

'A lot of people will disagree with this, but no vaccine, you can't go to the supermarket,' says the infamous CNN headline Don Lemon. 'No vaccine, no going to a game. No vaccine, no going to work. No vaccine, then you can't come here. No shirt, no shoes - no service,' referring to existing dress codes in restaurants, stores and businesses.

Lemon thinks that we 'should have this by now', because in his view it is a waste of effort to convince critical people. They go around in circles, they keep saying that it is their freedom, that it is whatever, 'I am free'. Lemon then uses the same fallacious and dangerously warped nonsense reasoning that you are not free to 'infect' others with a (supposed) disease, and that people also put liquor and other things into their bodies 'that are much worse than a vaccine.'

The body of another human being is ALWAYS inviolable

Yes, Don, but they do so voluntarily. No one is denying you the right to have this experimental gene therapy injected into your body, risking your health and life. So why do you want to deny others the right not to participate? Just because you think you're 'safer', when even official data shows that it makes no difference whether you've had the injections or not, and the authorities are now going to great lengths to conceal the fact that vaxxers are becoming much weaker and more vulnerable as a result?

'Neither Don Lemon nor other wage slaves of the mainstream media have any right to violate other people's bodies under threat of taking away their access to food and work. Even the suggestion that the government has (or should have) this right makes Lemon a fascist, a domestic enemy, someone who poses a very real threat to our civil rights,' Mike 'Natural

News' Adams comments. 'The medical fascists feel empowered to show their true colors.'

You still think that time is never going to come back and is even going to get much worse, as we have been writing for years? In Europe, we have already seen posts pass by on social media that are even more fascist than the medical rape that Don Lemon advocates. For example, some compatriots literally advocate putting unvaccinated people against the wall or gassing them "like the Jews.

Crimes against humanity

Legally, if someone tries to insert a sharp object into your body against your will, there is an intent to cause you serious bodily harm, and possibly even attempted murder. According to the Nürnberg code agreed upon after WW-2, people should never be forced to participate in medical experiments and treatments. Compulsory "vaccinations" - in this case experimental gene manipulation injections packaged as "vaccines" - therefore directly amount to a grave crime against humanity, to an attempt at mass murder, to genocide.

In my personal opinion, this also applies to the current non-compulsory injections, because people are persuaded under false pretences and with disinformation and lies to have these injections in their arms, and there is enormous pressure from politics, media and society to participate.

Anyone who, for whatever virtuous, humane or "scientific" sounding reason, is willing to sacrifice even one innocent life, is in his heart and soul an egotistical fascist with zero respect for the value of other human life. After all, this kind of thoughts and attitudes also made the Holocaust possible, because if you are willing to sacrifice one to make YOU feel 'safe', why not 10, 1000, a million, a billion?

'These vaccines are not there for public health, but for total control'

The well-known independent American analyst Brandon Smith is now convinced that the only reason for this massive vaccination campaign is to achieve total control over all humanity. To put that in prophetic perspective: to introduce the 'sign of the Beast' foretold in the Bible, without which no one will be able to 'buy or sell'.

'Why do they want 100% vaccinations? Why do they necessarily want every person in the world to get the mRNA shot?" writes Smith. 'Covid's average IFR is only 0.26% (recently adjusted by WHO to 0.15% - X.), which means that 99.7% of the public is NOT at risk, whether they are vaccinated or not... So these vaccines are NOT there for public health, nor for saving lives. They are overwhelmingly there for something else.'

'The mainstream media and globalists will claim that there is 'no evidence' that the mRNA causes lethal side effects or infertility. To that we would counter that there is NO PROOF that they are safe. Most vaccines are tested over the course of 10-15 years before they are used with the public. The Covid vaccines were introduced within a few months. Really, we have no desire to be used as a guinea pig for an untested vaccine.'

'Unvaccinated people will be proof of their crime'

'But what if the elite know exactly what these side effects will be? What if these vaccines are a key part of their 'Great Reset'?... In my mind, mass infertility is now being staged, for which Covid (or some variant) will be blamed, rather than the experimental vaccines. This is why the establishment wants a 100% vaccination rate; after all, unvaccinated people would be proof of their crime.' (See also our January 11 article: mRNA vaccines: genetic engineering is dangerous because it can cause infertility.)

'If millions of people remain unvaccinated over the next few years, then those will form a substantial and indisputable control group... If the vaccinated then get sick or die from specific diseases, and the control group doesn't suffer from them, then that's a pretty strong signal that your vaccine or drug is poison... If something goes wrong with the vaccines, then we will be the proof. we suspect this is what the elite are really afraid of.'

'They need to force us to get vaccinated too - ALL of us, so that there is no control group and no proof of what they have done. They can then simply blame Covid for the massive health problems, or some other bogus culprit.' (See also our June 21 article: Utopia: 2019 film predicted pandemic and vaccines covertly sterilizing world population (/ Shocking results of scientific study of hundreds of pregnant women: After Covid vaccination 82% spontaneous abortions in first 20 weeks of pregnancy).

'If the vaccines are a Trojan horse causing widespread disease or infertility, and the globalists are caught out because there is a control group, it will mean an outright revolt against them, complete with ropes and stakes. Their 'Great Reset' will fall apart. Which, by the way, given the many demonstrations and the huge backlash against vaccine passports, seems like it's going to happen anyway.

Who will win this endgame? The globalists or humanity?

'The globalists have set in motion an end game. That could mean the end game for us, but also for them. They are on a strict timeline. They need to get to 100% vaccination coverage in the next few years or sooner, implement their vaccine passports, and impose permanent lockdowns to quell growing discontent.'

'We are engaged in a race (against the clock) in which the globalists have to push their agenda through as quickly as possible, and we have to hold out and hold them back as long as possible, until the masses start to see the truth, which is that the lockdowns, obligations, and vaccines were never about safety, but always about control - from social control to population control.'

And if these injections are indeed doing what many independent scientists and experts have been warning about since last year, then population control is only the means to the great desired end of this global communist climate-vaccine cult, to which almost all Dutch politics seems to have bent its knees: population extermination, and on a scale that will completely dwarf the 100 to 150 million victims of Hitler, Stalin and Mao added together.

Chapter 9: News from 2009?

This is a flashback to a 2009 article discussing the possibility that the "Sign of the Beast" foretold in the Bible may well consist of a series of mandatory vaccinations with ingredients whose true effect and purpose will not be revealed until it is too late for everyone. Over the years we have written hundreds of articles on these topics, one of which we are again highlighting.

This article, too, is from 2009 (October 19), and was entitled "BEAST computer in Brussels ready to be activated.

Injection with nanochip planned 12 years ago?

October 19, 2009: One of America's best-known whistleblowers, Steve Quayle (say the 'Christian version' of Alex Jones), addresses his readers this week in a rather rare personal warning. 'In the past 24 hours -I am writing this on October 15- we have received confirmation from an Asian source that the bioweapon containing the nanochip located in the tip of the hypodermic needle is ready, and part of the supercomputer system in central Europe.'

'Although this sounds like a science fiction movie, unfortunately it is reality. In Belgium (Brussels) there is the BEAST (Beast) - Biometric Encryption And Satellite Tracking-, which is perfectly ready to be activated on the day that every living human being will be forced to accept the 'Sign of the Beast', in order to be admitted to the New World Order.'

'I call the genetically modified influenza vaccines, which are now being forced upon the public through a psychological operation that would be the envy of the greatest tyrants who ever lived, 'The Lucifer Virus' (lett. strain = lineage, nature, variant), because these vaccines have a far more evil side than most people can comprehend.'

'Ten years ago it was written that the ideal killing machine would be a genetically modified and altered vaccine, forcibly administered to the world's population under the pretext of "helping" them. I also argued that the U.S. military would be deliberately destroyed, not only by our enemies, but also by traitors in our own government, through the injection of a two-part bioweapon into our soldiers, with the second injection proving to be the death blow.'

'Through the mass media we heard the news that the German army is being administered a different vaccine than the ordinary civilian population (a vaccine without the extremely harmful adjuvants. we also received additional info that in the US, private military units - mercenaries - will be given a 'safe vaccine', different from the vaccine that will be given to ordinary people and soldiers in the army. However, it is against the Geneva Convention to use people as guinea pigs. For that reason, many Nazi doctors were sentenced to death.'

'Most dangerous period ever has arrived'

'The most dangerous period in all of history has arrived. Don't let these monsters destroy you, your children, your future and your lives. Do your homework. Read everything you can find about vaccines, get outraged, ask the right questions of all authorities. File charges, write letters, get on radio and TV programs. Do something! Do everything you can legally and morally do, because otherwise you may end up permanently in a horizontal position.'

Quayle prepared readers of his website (over 90 million hits a year) for a 'Red Screen' last week, as he expects the U.S. government to take all alternative news sites off the air at 'the right time'.

According to Quayle, this 'right moment' could be ushered in by, for example, total financial collapse, a nuclear 'attack', an EMP attack that will permanently knock out all electricity, a war in the Middle East, or a massive natural disaster such as a very large earthquake in the Midwest or a mega-tsunami on one of America's coasts.

In our opinion, this warning should be viewed both seriously and soberly. It is clear that "something" is about to happen, but how, where and when, that can only be speculated on at this time based on clues and developments.

The Lucifer Virus

July 31, 2021: The hyped swine flu 'pandemic' in 2009 turned out in retrospect to be weaker than a normal seasonal flu, and was a kind of dress rehearsal for what has been going on around the world since 2020, again under the guise of a (supposed) respiratory virus with an IFR of only 0.15%, and 0.05% (= half of a typical seasonal flu) if you are under 70 years old.

Quayle called a genetically modified vaccine the "Lucifer Virus" because "these vaccines have a much more malignant side than most people can contain. As is well known, the Covid-19 vaccinations are in reality not 'vaccines' but mRNA gene manipulation injections, a fact that was openly announced in the Government Gazette last year.

Recently, university scientists in Spain discovered graphene oxide in Pfizer vaccines, which is not mentioned either on the package insert or in the official EMA documents. Do the Covid injections perhaps contain even more hidden 'malicious' ingredients, such as foreign (manipulated) RNA/DNA? Since 2009 we have devoted entire article series to this possibility. In the near future we may bring them to your attention again with a number of summarizing flashbacks.

Since the government has also given official permission for you and your (grand)children to be genetically manipulated with experimental injections, it seems that it cannot be excluded that these also contain substances and/or mRNA instructions that code your body for something other than just the officially stated reason, namely to create the spike protein of the so-called 'novel' coronavirus.

Considering the enormous numbers of deaths and illnesses that the Covid injections have officially caused already - the tip of the iceberg, because most cases are deliberately not recorded - the term 'Lucifer Virus', 'Lucifer Vaccine' or 'Lucifer Injection' might prove to be quite appropriate, especially if in the coming months and years millions of people are affected by blood clots, ADEs and all kinds of serious illnesses.

Confused behavior of vaccinated people?

In recent months we have been told by several unvaccinated contacts that some vaccinated people in their environment are exhibiting 'strange behavior', especially a form of absence and lethargy, and can hardly follow or understand simple facts and logical arguments anymore.

Is this just coincidence, perception, or perhaps the result of the damage to the red blood cells demonstrated by the Covid injections, which reduces the amount of oxygen transported through the body?

Or is there perhaps more to it, something attributable to any secret ingredients?

Nanotech biosensor in Covid vaccines?

Whether or not a literal 'BEAST' supercomputer has been built in Brussels is really irrelevant. A few years ago, in the American state of Utah, a monstrous data center was built (UDC) that functions exactly like a BEAST, and controls a 'Global Information Grid' in which truly ALL public and personal digital information of every world citizen, conversations, e-mails, transactions, payments - right down to parking tickets - is stored. To make this possible, the UDC's computers achieve a speed of 1 petaflop (10 to the 15th power) of calculations per second. (Chances are that speed is much higher by now).

On January 23, 2013 an article called: 'EU wants to introduce a total surveillance system for citizens, just like the US' with a reference to this (officially never recognized) BEAST supercomputer in Brussels: 'EU citizens could in the near future be secretly equipped with a nanochip under the guise of vaccinations against, for example, a flu epidemic, which would allow them to be tracked and monitored 24/7/365 by the BEAST system.

Could this have become a reality some 8 years later? In this regard, read our September 3, 2020 article: 'Implantable 5G nanotech biosensor as early as 2021 in

61

Covid-19 vaccines' and consider that WEF top man Klaus Schwab in his book 'The Great Reset' has announced an 'Internet of Bodies', and as a possible precursor already in the next few years wants to introduce a mandatory electronic bracelet, which is in direct contact with your body and which in addition to your location and activity also records your health, including whether or not you have received 'vaccinations'.

Without 'chip' / vaccination, you will soon not be allowed to do anything at all

The article about 'GPS in smartphones precursor to implanted chip' (23 October 2013) explains it as follows: 'When it is considered that in the future, without a microchip, we may not be able to do anything -not be able to buy, sell, live, receive salary/benefits, be denied access anywhere- then refusing such a chip seems to become an impossible task for most people indeed.'

Replace 'microchip' with vaccination (passport), and you have exactly what more and more politicians worldwide are now openly announcing and even already deciding, such as Philippine President Duterte, who has said he will use the police to keep unvaccinated people permanently locked up at home.

Bizarrely, many are still in deep denial about this. How much more evidence does it take to make people realize that the dreaded totalitarian future we have been warning about since 2008 is unfortunately becoming a reality?

Chapter 10: Covid fascist tyranny

France and other Western countries on the brink of revolutions? - British newborn babies subjected to mandatory PCR test - Australia deploys army; 'Sydney turned into concentration camp' - Are you now also 'compromised beyond repair'?

We have been warning for many years that the 1930s and 1940s are on repeat and are even in danger of being far surpassed in horror and inhumanity. That was something most people could not yet imagine. Surely by mid-2021 that should have changed, as governments around the world rapidly impose rock-hard fascist Covid tyranny on their populations. However, they can only do this because the majority of people - despite the huge load of evidence of the constant lies and deceptions - are still blindly following the corona pandemic propaganda.

Italy: Anti-Green Pass protest in parliament

In Italy, a number of opposition members protested in parliament with signs reading "Say NO to Green Pass. For a moment there seemed to be chaos and panic. In the southern European country, large freedom demonstrations against Covid policies take place with regularity, as they did in Milan.

Will there still be new elections?

New elections will take place in Germany on September 26, and in France in June 2022. Will these still take place? 'There are rumors that various government leaders realize they are being voted out, and are talking seriously about "suspending" all elections as long as this "pandemic" exists,' writes American economist Martin Armstrong. In Canada, a bill was already introduced in June to do exactly that and thus end democracy. It is also possible that election results will simply be falsified, as happened in the US at the end of last year.

(In the Netherlands, democracy has long since ended, and a totalitarian acting regime is in power that, despite its caretaker status, keeps making very far-reaching decisions, and is barely challenged in the process. (While simple matters like improving a traffic junction are declared 'controversial'! Talk about the upside-down world).

The French have patently lost all faith in politics. In elections in June, President Macron's left-liberal party received only 10.9% of the vote. Marine Le Pen's RN got 19.1%, and the Republicans 29.3%. A whopping 68% didn't bother to vote. The people are never listened to anyway, and the real decisions are made in Brussels (EU) and Davos (World Economic Forum).

'Even Louis XVI, who was beheaded, had the support of more people than Macron. Given the panic cycles that appear in our election models in 2022, this is clearly not a domestic issue. The last time this happened was when

Roosevelt and Hitler were elected.' 'Our models for France wise up on September 23/24'.

Philippine city: unvaccinated should just starve to death

Macron recently announced that unvaccinated people will soon be denied access to public transport and shopping malls, and healthcare workers will be required to be vaccinated. This caused massive protests in dozens of cities. Hundreds of thousands took to the streets, but of course the Dutch media kept quiet about it. (They only come out with all the cameras and journalists they can get if a handful of climate extremists or Black Lives Matter activists are demonstrating somewhere).

The mayor of the Philippine city Lapu-Lapu has gone one step further than the French president and barred unvaccinated people from entering all supermarkets, grocery stores and other food stores. In other words: no shot? Then starve to death.

British hospital threatens parents who refuse to submit expectant baby to PCR test

Great Britain is also sinking at breakneck speed into heavenly inhuman Covid madness and insanity. A hospital is threatening to take measures against parents-to-be because they refuse to submit their babies to a PCR test after birth. Yep: even newborns must be subjected to the utterly pointless and potentially harmful PCR test.

Conservative MP Graham Brady, chairman of the Tory 1922 committee, wrote in an op-ed in the Daily Mail that there is only one real reason for the lockdowns: social control, and not countering Covid. He even compared today's society to Stockholm Syndrome: the greater the control to which people are subjected, the more dependent they become.

'Sydney turned into concentration camp'

In Australia - where there are also new elections in 2022 - the police are now given complete free rein to enforce the fifth strangling lockdown, whereby you end up in jail if you go further than 5 km. from your home. A few thousand people ventured out to protest (which is strictly prohibited and gets you arrested in New South Wales), but they were quickly dealt with harshly.

The government even announced it would use the army. And why? Because of a whopping TWO new Covid deaths in Sydney, one aged 90 and one aged 80. A quarter of those over 70 are still not 'vaccinated', and this is being called 'unacceptable'.

No mouth guard on - $500 fine, even for vaccinated people. The police can close any store if it is thought that the rules are not being followed. 'They've turned Sydney into a concentration camp,' Armstrong comments. 'They tell people that the sooner they get vaccinated, the sooner their freedom will be restored. They tell people to snitch on their neighbors, which was exactly the same tactic of the Stasi in East Germany.'

'Civilization beyond repair'

'The long-term consequences of these measures will completely break society, because once you turn neighbors against each other, you cannot restore civilization. Orders are being issued all over the world to turn society upside down and make people at each other's throats.'

As will soon be the case in the United States? There the CDC has now openly stated that it is mainly the fully vaccinated who are spreading the (supposed) Delta and Lambda variants. Meanwhile, the media is falsely blaming only the unvaccinated, which means that the deliberately stirred up hatred between these groups may at some point degenerate into brute force.

Armstrong: "And there's the risk that we'll have a real version of The Hunger Games, now that Biden is paying farmers NOT to grow crops. Is this why (Bill) Gates has become the biggest landowner in the U.S. - to stop food production?'

Western governments and parliaments 'no longer represent the people'

With human rights being trampled even in Western countries, 'there will be revolutions,' Armstrong warns. 'Our computer is very clear about that. Our current form of governments and parliaments will collapse, because they no longer represent the people.' The policemen who collaborate in suppressing their own citizens 'will forever be seen by history as evil tyrants. Just because a politician commands something does NOT make it legal, ethical or morally right.'

'We must ask why the police use the same excuse as the Nazis did in World War II: 'Befehl is Befehl'. This means that they are incapable of actually thinking freely.

'The computer (the A.I. 'Socrates') designated August to October as a dark period when there will be an all-out attack on the unvaccinated. we hate to see this come true. A civilization arises when it is to the advantage of all to work together. Civilizations collapse when divisions emerge, and that is exactly what governments worldwide are now doing to stay in power. History warns that they will fail in that process. Perhaps now you will understand how Socrates also predicted that nations will divide along the same lines as they did during previous conflicts.'

Is Klaus Schwab's cyber attack coming?

'(Klaus) Schwab may be twisting the social unrest by claiming that people want his communist solution and 'equality', but he is deliberately carrying out this

69

deception in order to subject the whole world to his economic vision. Sooner or later, the people will also storm the World Economic Forum. 'In September, tempers will get even more heated,' Armstrong thinks.

Will that be the time when Klaus Schwabs orders his announced and recently rehearsed (false flag) cyber attack, designed to finally deliver the final blow to the Western people, economy and civilization, and subjugate them to the harshest communist dictatorship ever? Armstrong recently called Schwab and Gates, who seem to see themselves as some sort of untouchable demigods, literally the new Hitlers. we personally think that the misery that both gentlemen are creating - with the full agreement and/or cooperation of almost all 'our' politicians and members of parliament - will make Hitler a choirboy.

Chapter 11: Passports & chips

A 2016 interview with WEF senior executive Klaus Schwab, in which he predicts that "within 10 years" an obligatory global health card will be adopted, and everyone will have implanted microchips, adds to the proof that the Covid-19 issue was painstakingly prepared.

Schwab was reportedly working on a plan at least five years ago to create a huge virus outbreak and exploit it to establish health passports and link them to mandatory testing and vaccinations, all according to the problem-reaction-solution approach. The goal is to have complete control over the whole human population on the planet.

'Within 10 years, we will have implanted microchips,' said Schwab five years ago.

In 2016, a French-speaking interviewer asked him, 'Are we talking about implantable chips?' 'When is it going to happen?'

'Absolutely in the next ten years,' said Schwab. 'We'll start by putting them in our clothes.' We can next picture implanting them in our brains or skin.' The WEF foreman then commented on his vision of man and machine 'fusing.'

'In the future, we may be able to communicate directly between our brains and the digital world.' We observe a merger of the physical, digital, and biological worlds.' People will simply have to think about someone in the future to be able to reach them straight through the 'cloud.'

There will be no more biological persons with natural DNA in the transhumanist world, which will finally become fully "digital." The 'cloud' will be used to store everyone's data.

Humanity has begun to be reprogrammed genetically.

The current economic order will be destroyed by Schwab's 'Great Reset' ('Build Back Better'). The looming financial meltdown will be exploited to launch a new global system based only on digital money and transactions. This new system will be connected to the entire world thanks to 5G technology. Refusers will be barred from "buying and selling," in other words, from social life.

In the late 2020s, Covid-19 mRNA 'vaccines' began genetically programming and manipulating humanity in order to make it 'fit' to be first linked, then integrated, with this global digital system, which, as you know, we believe is the Biblical realm of 'the Beast.'

These gene-altering vaccines have the potential to eliminate your free will and ability to think for yourself, as well as your desire and ability to connect with the spiritual realm.

Christian Perspective: Humanity is cut off from God

From a Christian perspective, the reprogramming of human DNA through these vaccines can be seen as Satan's final attempt to permanently separate humankind from God. This appears to be the true explanation for the prophetic Bible book of Revelation's warning that individuals who bear this "mark" will perish.

This isn't simply because of a chip and a succession of pricks; it's because of what those pricks will do to and in you. As a result, God will be unable to save those whose minds (free will) have been reprogrammed to total obedience ('worship'). That will necessitate His intervention, for otherwise, humanity as a whole will be lost forever.

False teachings have blinded a large portion of Christianity.

The essential aspect of this devious plot, which has been in the works for a long time, was the infiltration of Christianity with a series of false teachings, with the goal of keeping believers blind until the end of time in preparation for the advent and establishment of the Beast's rule.

Indeed, tens to hundreds of millions of Christians, particularly in the West, believe that they will never have to live through this period. Even now, when the implementation of this system has begun, the majority of people refuse to accept it. With their pro-vaccination views, most Christian parties and churches are openly cooperating in this "Great Reset" to the domain of "the Beast." In theological terms, the Vatican is the most powerful and convinced driver of this.

'But we were duped!' isn't an excuse.

Perhaps a biblical parallel can help some people understand? Genesis 3, the tale of creation and the 'Fall,' as told to us today: The serpent persuaded Adam and Eve that they were not allowed to 'eat' the 'apple,' in this case the sign, i.e. not to have it pricked in them (root test of 'the sign': charagma = scratch/something with a needle = prick), but the serpent persuaded them that this sign would not damn them, but rather make them into 'gods.' After being persuaded by this falsehood, their complaints against God ('but we've been lied to!') were futile, and they died slowly and painfully. They could have and should have known, thus they had no justification.

Accepting 'the sign,' according to the Bible, carries an even worse consequence: eternal death. Allowing yourself to be genetically modified with mRNA vaccinations and then integrated into a global digital network, so relinquishing all control over your body and free will, will be up to each individual to decide whether the danger is worth it.

Some doctors are so indoctrinated and terrified that they blame the sick themselves: 'My employer put a lot of pressure on me to be vaccinated.'

The Highwire, the fastest growing American Internet health program that already has more than 75 million viewers, recently focused attention on a troubling trend in the U.S. that may also be occurring in other Western countries. In fact, more and more doctors are refusing to treat people who suffer from serious side effects and adverse reactions after vaccination with a Covid-19 vaccine. The reason is obvious: the political and pharmaceutical establishment has effectively canonized these gene-manipulated vaccines. If people do get very sick or even die from them - in the U.S. in 2021 there will already be 4000% more vaccine victims than in the whole of 2020 from all other vaccinations combined - then the instructions are that it cannot and must not be the vaccine's fault. Doctors who nevertheless observe this must fear for their jobs and careers.

Some doctors are so indoctrinated that they blame the sick themselves. They call people who suffer serious side effects after vaccination patients with a 'conversion disorder', afraid to put in their file that the vaccine is the probable cause. (Or, in other words, 'go back home, little lady, because it's between your ears.')

'On January 4, I was put under great pressure by my
employer to get vaccinated,' Shawn Skelton told me.
After she complied, she immediately experienced side
effects such as mild flu-like symptoms. 'But by the end
of the day, my legs were hurting so badly that I couldn't
take it anymore. When I woke up the next day my
tongue was twitching, and then it got worse and worse.
The next day I had convulsions all over my body. That
lasted 13 days.'

'Too afraid to treat us,' they say.

'One doctor told me the diagnosis was, 'I don't know
what's wrong with you, therefore we blame you,'" said
another. Skelton elaborated. 'Doctors just do not know
how to address the mRNA vaccine's negative effects. I
also believe they are terrified of it. I'm at a loss for
words as to why no doctor wants to help us.'

Two other healthcare workers, Angelia Desselle and
Kristi Simmonds had similar experiences. They too
suffered convulsions, and their doctors also refused to
treat them. A neurologist rejected Desselle's email
referral to him. 'He was a movement disorder specialist,
which I thought I needed. My primary care physician
said it looked like I had advanced Parkinson's. But he
emailed back that he had very complex duties, and he
couldn't see me at that time.'

As other doctors likewise kept the door closed to her,
she went to a neurologist without mentioning that she

had been vaccinated against Covid-19. 'I didn't want to be sent away again. But it is in my medical record, so when he looked at that he said 'so you took the vaccine?' And I said 'yes, but I didn't want to give you that information because I need help.' Now she is finally receiving treatment for her migraine attacks.
In Europe, general practitioners and specialists are subject to stringent regulations.

We don't know if general practitioners in Europe also refuse to treat vaccinated patients who become unwell. They are, however, prohibited from prescribing proven-effective and safe drugs to (suspected) corona patients, such as hydroxychloroquine and Ivermectin. Nothing should threaten the "holy" mass vaccination program - recovery: genetic engineering program, after all.

In Europe, general practitioners and specialists are subject to stringent regulations.

We don't know if general practitioners in Europe also refuse to treat vaccinated patients who become unwell. They are, however, prohibited from prescribing proven-effective and safe drugs to (suspected) corona patients, such as hydroxychloroquine and Ivermectin. Nothing should threaten the "holy" mass vaccination program - recovery: genetic engineering program, after all.

Earlier this year, the government put any responsibility for the consequences of the Covid vaccinations on the shoulders of health care providers and the people who are vaccinated with them. It is therefore not inconceivable that healthcare professionals and specialists in Europe will be reluctant to recognize, let alone treat, vaccination victims as such.

Chapter 13: Super variants

'So-called experts who claim that the variants are caused by unvaccinated people have no scientific understanding whatsoever. The only real cause is mass vaccination. These vaccines suppress the natural immunity of vaccinated people'

The eminent vaccine expert Dr. Geert Vanden Bossche, who previously worked with the GAVI alliance and the Bill & Melinda Gates Foundation, has published an article with the telling title 'Last Warning. If the world does not immediately stop Covid vaccinations now, he is convinced an unstoppable wave of serious, incurable and deadly illnesses will be upon us.

Vanden Bossche is a systems scientist who is normally very pro-vaccination, and therefore still assumes the existence of the 'novel' corona / SARS-CoV-2 virus and proven 'infections'. We'll leave that debatable position for now, because right now the most important thing is for politicians to stop ignoring the growing opposition of established scientists like him.

Earlier this year, Vanden Bossche warned that providing billions of people with new vaccines during a pandemic - an absolute no go in immunology until 2020 - could have dire consequences because it could make the mutations that normally always occur, especially of respiratory viruses like corona, much more dangerous.

'These vaccinations have the opposite effect'

In his 'Final Warning' article, he sets out with extensive scientifically based arguments that exactly what he was so afraid of is now happening. The mainstream media is falsely trying to blame the unvaccinated for the new variants and related measures. This is something the vaccine expert vehemently opposes.

His long technical story boils down to the fact that it is precisely the Covid-19 vaccinations that cause some mutations to become resistant to immunity. 'Mass vaccination campaigns during a pandemic, especially during a pandemic with more infectious variants, will neither achieve group immunity nor contain future waves of disease... In fact, they have the exact opposite effect by promoting the spread of stronger VI escape variants, and suppressing natural immunity in vaccinated persons.' (emphasis added)

'This will only lead to higher morbidity and mortality rates in that part of the population that normally has natural protection against Covid-19 (or the vast majority of the population). A decrease in severe morbidity and mortality is only seen in the elderly and in those with some underlying diseases. Therefore, the result of the mass vaccination campaigns is totally different from the original goal, which was to protect the vast majority of people.'

'Severe consequences due to super variants if we continue to vaccinate'

Scientifically, he says, it is hardly conceivable that more contagious SARS-CoV-2 variants will not rapidly escape the immunity that large portions of humanity have already developed, 'and pass into a supervariant that evades the immune response of all S-based (spike) Covid-19 vaccines. It is simply inconceivable that ongoing mass vaccination campaigns can contain, let alone end, these pandemic or more contagious SARS-CoV-2 variants, and force this virus to acquire milder characteristics, rather than more problematic ones.'

These new variants 'pose a huge and immediate threat to the human population, and will have dire consequences if we continue mass vaccination during these high infection rates, while prevention measures are largely relaxed.'

'Mass vaccination is the only real culprit'

'Last but not least, it must be emphasized that those who call themselves "experts" and pretend that this pandemic is a "pandemic of the unvaccinated" have no scientific understanding whatsoever of the evolutionary dynamics of Sars-CoV-2, as it is now emerging from a combination of high viral infectivity and the (high) rate of vaccination.' (underlined and bold added)

'Neither the vaccinated (who merely believed that the vaccine would protect them from Covid-19) nor the unvaccinated (who simply believe that they do not need a vaccine to remain protected) can be blamed for this escalation of the pandemic. Mass vaccination is the only real culprit.'

(A copy of this letter was sent to the WHO, NIH, CDC, Bill & Melinda Gates Foundation, GAVI, FDA, EMEA, and to the R&D leaders of Pfizer, Moderna, Astra-Zeneca, J&J, Novavax, and GSK).

Chapter 12: Immune system suppression

Covid-19 is "mainly a vascular illness," according to researchers - Circulation Research: Lung injury is aided by spike protein - Your immune system is working against you to protect you from the vaccine.

In a scientific publication, researchers at the famed Salk Institute, which was founded by vaccine pioneer Jonas Salk, indirectly admit that the Covid vaccinations induce life-threatening blood clots and harm to both blood vessels and the immune system.

We noted earlier this week that an increasing number of well-known scientists are coming to the opinion that vaccines are the greatest hazard to human health.

Thousands of Europeans and Americans have already paid with their lives, and hundreds of thousands with their health, for their "voluntary" participation in history's greatest "medical" experiment.

In the West, all Covid vaccinations program the human body to create the spike protein, the most lethal element of the alleged SARS-CoV-2 virus, with the goal of shielding humans against the spike protein's damaging consequences.

In a nutshell, we make your body manufacture something harmful in order for it to generate antibodies against that same danger, but we have no idea how or if this process will ever be stopped.

So why not take the "risk" of getting the virus, which has been shown to not make 99.7% of the population sick, if at all? No, in 2021, that rational, historically uncontroversial line of reasoning is suddenly so antiquated. We can no longer rely on our natural immune system and must instead rely on what is administered through a syringe.

'Covid-19 is mostly a vascular illness,' says the researcher.

The vaccination industry, politicians, and the media continue to insist that the spike protein is safe, but the Salk Institute has now established that this is not the case. On the contrary, the Salk researchers and other scientific colleagues warn in the publication "The spike protein of the new coronavirus plays an extra crucial role in disease" that the spike protein harms cells, "confirming that Covid-19 is largely a vascular illness."

Another spike protein that has claimed so many lives?

Of course, the Salk scientists are forbidden from criticizing vaccines directly. That is why, according to their article, the spike protein produced by vaccines behaves quite differently than the spike protein produced by the alleged virus.

To begin with, this contradicts all vaccine makers' claims that their vaccines create the same spike protein. Second, it casts doubt on the efficacy of vaccines, because if the spike protein produced by vaccines differs significantly from that produced by the virus, what is the point of vaccination (assuming, for the time being, that these genetically designed 'vaccines' operate at all)?

On the plus side, even pro-vaccine scientists now accept that the spike protein is to blame for a large number of deaths and people suffering from major side effects and long-term, often permanent health harm. In other words, it's an implied admission that Covid-19 vaccinations are potentially fatal.

Spike protein causes lung injury, according to research published in Circulation Research.

"The SARS-Cov-2 spike protein impairs endothelial function by inhibiting ACE-2," according to a scientific study published in Circulation Research. The inside of the heart and blood vessels are lined with edothele cells. By decreasing ACE-2 receptors, the spike protein 'promotes lung injury.' The endothelial cells in blood arteries are damaged, and the metabolism is disrupted as a result.

The authors of this study were also pro-vaccination, claiming that "vaccine-generated antibodies" may protect the body from the spike protein. Essentially, the spike protein can cause significant damage to vascular cells, and the immune system can counteract this damage by fighting the spike protein.

The immune system is trying to protect you AGAINST the vaccine

In other words, the human immune system strives to defend the patient from the vaccine's negative effects and counter-reactions in order to prevent the patient from dying. Anyone who survives the Covid vaccine owes it to their own immune system's protection AGAINST the vaccine, not the vaccination itself.

'The vaccination is the weapon,' Mike 'Natural News' Adams concludes. 'Your immune system protects you. All Covid vaccinations should be withdrawn off the market immediately and re-evaluated for long-term negative effects based on this research alone.'

According to official VAERS statistics, the number of vaccine-related deaths in the United States in 2021 will be almost 4000 percent more than the total number of vaccine-related deaths in 2020.

The holy vaccine is not to blame for a heart attack or a cerebral hemorrhage.

The following mechanism has been scientifically proved and is now established: the Covid-19 vaccinations encourage your body to make the spike protein, which can cause vascular damage and blood clots, which can move throughout the body and end up in various organs (heart, lungs, brain, etc.). People who die as a result of this are referred to as having had a "heart attack," "blood clot," or "brain haemorrhage" - the sacrosanct vaccines can and must never be blamed, no matter how much evidence there is today showing they are the main reasons.

Vaccine recipients appear to offer a risk to the unvaccinated, in addition to the possibility for permanent or deadly harm to their own health. Many of the corona'wappies' who have recently had their shots have been transformed into walking'spike factories,' and can now exhale these spike proteins. They can so infect others through this 'shedding' process.

Bioweapon vaccines were created by the apartheid administration against the black population.

Vaccines have long been used as bioweapons against the general public. South Africa's Apartheid Government created the technology underlying such a "self-replicating" vaccination. Scientists were developing 'racial' vaccines at the time, with the goal of eradicating much of the black population.

This year, the Johns Hopkins Bloomberg School of Public Health proposed using a self-replicating vaccine to automatically 'vaccinate' the whole world's population.

Drones and AI robots would subsequently be used to enforce and monitor the program.

People who are still eager to sign up in a vaccine alley to be genetically modified to generate a potentially life-threatening spike protein appear to have been fully misled by the mainstream media and system politicians. They've been numb to all the warnings and the mountains of proof, and they can't believe the world is being ruled by unscrupulous monsters who have no qualms about committing the potentially single biggest genocide in human history.

Chapter 14: Fear propaganda

Government 'has mass of innocent souls on its conscience' - 'Don't believe their lies' as government and media come out with new alarmist statements

The editor-in-chief of Europe's largest newspaper, Germany's Bild, asked the public's forgiveness on camera for the fear propaganda about Covid-19. 'We convinced our children that they would kill their grandmother if they dared to be what they are: children. Or if they met their friends. None of this has been scientifically proven.' He warned the government that with the harsh lockdown measures, it will go down in the history books as leaders who will have 'a mass of innocent souls on their conscience.'

The coverage in Bild 'has been like poison,' editor-in-chief Julian Reichelt admitted on camera. It has given children 'the feeling that you were a lethal danger to society,' with now proven highly damaging psychological effects around the world, and in many countries a sharply increased number of suicides.

'Forgive us that this policy has made you victims for a year and a half'

'To the millions of children in this country for whom our society is responsible, I would like to testify here what neither our government nor our chancellor dares to tell you. We ask you to forgive us. Forgive us for this policy that has made you victims of violence, neglect, isolation and loneliness for a year and a half.'

'We have convinced our children that they would kill their grandmother if they dared to be what they are: children. Or if they met their friends. None of this has been scientifically proven. If a state takes away a child's rights, it must prove that doing so protects the child from concrete and immediate danger. That proof has never been provided. It has been replaced by propaganda by which the child has been presented as a vector of the pandemic.'

'Don't believe their lies'

Reichelt also pointed to the fact that experts with other, more moderate views 'were never invited to the table.' The editor-in-chief urged everyone to 'not believe these lies' when the government and media once again come up with all kinds of alarmist statements (about variants, (fake) 'infections', etc.).

The top man of the newspaper, which with 1.24 million copies is the largest in Europe, called on the authorities to reopen schools and sports halls immediately, and warned the politicians that with their harsh lockdown measures they will go down in the history books as leaders who will have "a mass of innocent souls on their conscience.

Europe turned into harsh dictatorship

Tens of thousands of demonstrators protesting in Berlin against the introduction of vaccination passports and the discrimination against and exclusion of the unvaccinated were savagely attacked by the police. The shocking images were not inferior to the harshest fascist dictatorships that have ever existed on this planet. This prompted UN Special Rapporteur on Torture Nils Melzer to ask eyewitnesses to come forward for a possible official investigation into serious human rights violations.

It was recently revealed that the German intelligence service is monitoring and spying on anti-lockdown protesters, claiming they are part of a "conspiracy" to "disrupt" society. The European government recently passed a law that makes it possible to treat all other opinions and dissenting voices as 'disruptive to society'. This was the umpteenth proof that our country too is being turned into a totalitarian fascist dictatorship by our own leaders.

Chapter 15: No vaccine = no civil rights

'These outrages: Your fault! You have been quietly watching and silently tolerating. This is your great fault: you are partly responsible for these heinous crimes!' Then about the fate of the Jews, later about the fate of the unvaccinated?

As early as January 2020, before 'corona' even arrived inEurope, we wrote that the so-called 'pandemic' could well be a pretext for the establishment of a tyrannical world government in which our freedom, democracy and self-determination will have come to a complete end. Although most people refused to believe that it would ever come to that, we repeated this warning many times. With good reason, because just look at the full blown fascist Apartheid measures being taken in Europe. Like in Italy, where unvaccinated people are now denied access to polling stations, and unvaccinated politicians and parliamentarians are no longer allowed on the Democratic Party's candidate list.

Under item 8 of the World Economic Forum's "The Great Reset," flowery terms about supposedly upholding human rights announce the end of our democracy. If it were up to Klaus Schwab, nobody would have any say whatsoever about their own life, future, health and even body. As we know, Sigrid Kaag and Mark Rutte, who literally described Schwab's Great Reset as 'a hopeful future', are fully behind this long-planned, and now in progress, technocratic coup against our society and future.

No vaccine = no vote

Italian Prime Minister Mario Draghi, who as ECB President single-handedly hammered a hefty nail into the coffin of the Eurozone with years of negative interest rates, shows what this real agenda of the Covid pledge and all its restrictive measures is. Now that the Covid passport has been officially introduced in the EU, Draghi is taking the next tyrannical step by making this passport mandatory not only for restaurants, events and public transport, but also for access to polling stations. In other words, no prick = no vote.

Former Prime Minister Enrico Letta (2013-2014) of the Democratic Party PD, also president of the extremist pro-EU think tank Institut Jacques Delors, has meanwhile announced that unvaccinated people will no longer be included on the list of candidates. It is only a matter of time before the other parties in parliament, and then other EU countries, follow suit.

'100% vaccinations to enforce total obedience'

The Europeans may 'not have firearms, but they can fight back in other ways,' comments American economist Martin Armstrong. 'These leaders are so derailed and emotionless because they can no longer keep up the pretence that they have everything under control. They can no longer finance their debts, and cannot conceive of ever stopping spending.'

'They are changing the economy for the Great Reset BECAUSE the system is failing. The real goal of 100% vaccinations is to turn the whole society into obedient drones '.

'Covid tyrants will revert to slaughtering people'

'These Covid tyrants will simply have to fall back on slaughtering people.' Thus, throughout the West, freedom protesters everywhere are being savagely attacked - as was the case a few days ago in Berlin, when even old women were thrown to the ground by the M.E. and a 48-year-old woman was beaten to death with batons - and portrayed by the media as dangerous extremists, insurgents, 'dangers to society' and even terrorists and enemies of the state.

If you think: where is this going, just reread the historical annals about the Nazis' persecution of the Jews in the 1930s. Replace 'Jews' with 'Unvaccinated', and see for yourself the chilling similarities. Like the Jews at the time, non- and anti-vaxxers are beginning to lose not only their freedoms, but also their jobs and positions. (See also our September 23, 2020 article: This is how Reichsmarschall Göring got the people to do it: 'Scare them and tell them that refusers are a danger').

If people do not peacefully rise up en masse against this state discrimination, inhumane exclusion and Apartheid, unvaccinated people will eventually be completely ostracized from society. Then a new 'final solution' is also looming around the corner: concentration camps.

Who is silent, agrees

'These outrages: Your fault! You have quietly stood by and silently tolerated. This is your great fault: you are partly responsible for these atrocious crimes!" read a poster distributed in Germany shortly after the war in 1945, showing some shocking photographs of entire piles of emaciated corpses of Jews.

Indifferent then to the fate of the Jews, indifferent now to the fate of the unvaccinated? Given the attitude of politicians and the scandalously biased reporting in the mainstream and social media (01-08: CNN openly calls for all the unvaccinated to starve to death), things are moving hard in that direction. As I've concluded articles many times before: humanity has learned absolutely nothing from the past, and is making EXACTLY the same fatal mistakes again as it did then. Only the number of victims of Schwab, Gates, Soros and all their political lackeys will be a multiple of those of Hitler, Stalin, Lenin and Mao added together.

Nevertheless, there is still time for a mass peaceful NO. At the same time, in our entire post-war history, now

96

more than ever before, the rule is: he who is silent, agrees. Or has the conscience of the people and its leaders already been dulled to such an extent that the end of all freedom and this exclusion and expulsion of the unvaccinated, leading to an Endlösung, is actually considered a fine idea?

Chapter 16: Vaccine subscriptions?

Researchers from the 'Virus Watch' division of University College London (UCL) have concluded that the Covid-19 vaccines lose their supposed protective effect after only 6 weeks. This means that every vaccinated person will have to receive new 'booster shots' every 2 or 3 months, making the 'vaccine subscription' we predicted over a year ago a reality. Blood tests show time and again that the vaccines alter and damage red blood cells, causing them to clump. In most vaccinated people, it takes several months to a few years at most before they begin to experience serious effects from this.

Blood analysis of 552 'vaccinated' people, mainly aged 50 to 70, showed that the antibodies allegedly produced by the Pfizer and AstraZeneca vaccines began to decline after only a month and a half. In some, the so-called 'vaccine immunity' is reduced by more than half in less than 3 months.

Despite total failure, 'vaccinations' continue

Since last year, the population has been bombarded by the mainstream media with propaganda that up to two injections would protect you from Covid-19. Critical scientists and other experts immediately pointed out that this is most likely great nonsense. They were reviled for it as 'disinformation' spreaders, but now appear to have been proven right yet again.

Despite this total failure of their "holy" injections, the vaccine believers will not budge. Eleanor Riley, Professor of Immunology at Edinburgh University, for example, claims that the results were 'expected', and 'not necessarily a problem'.

No, not if the intention from the outset was to give people 'booster shots' to infinity. These, she claims, would be 'necessary' to reduce the 'spread' of the disease, a claim for which, incidentally, there is still no evidence.

Permanently on the booster shots

On the contrary: there is increasing evidence that the Covid injections cause the very "variants" that the media falsely blame on the unvaccinated, and that the vaccinated are extra vulnerable to them because of the injections. At the same time, a new study shows that naturally built-up immunity (i.e. without vaccination) most likely does offer lifelong protection.

The experimental mRNA gene therapy injections, packaged as 'vaccines', are at best a fantastic new business model for Big Pharma. With the help of unsuspecting or unscrupulous politicians, force the entire world population to have permanent booster shots injected into their bodies, and then also earn billions from the many (chronic) diseases and disorders that people get as a result.

30% to 60% already have formation blood clots

And that this is going to happen is actually a given. Various studies among vaccinated people in Germany and Canada, among others, showed that at least 30% to over 60% are already developing blood clots. Even extremely healthy young people developed myocarditis and pericarditis after vaccination. A major reason for this is clogged blood vessels, capillaries and veins.

We recently calculated that if the findings of (general) practitioners in Germany, Canada and Great Britain are internationally normative, between 150,000 and 400,000 citizens for a small country will die from blood clots in the next few years.

The British doctor Dr. Van Welbergen, with more than 40 years of experience, had the blood of his patients who had been injected with Moderna examined under the microscope. The results were shocking: numerous red blood cells were found to be damaged, so that they no longer flow 'smoothly' through the blood vessels, but began to clump.

'This is unimaginably mind-boggling and frightening,' said Dr Ruby. 'We now know that the Pfizer and Moderna vaccines are the cause of blood clots and all these brain haemorrhages and heart attacks, the myocarditis, the weakness, the neurological disorders similar to guillain-barré and MS.... The blood looks poisoned. There are dangerous things in it, and the red blood cells react violently to it and get disrupted.' As a result, oxygen is no longer transported properly through the body, causing people to become tired, dizzy, absent-minded, confused, etc.

'Crimes against humanity under pretext of vaccinations'

Meanwhile, more and more vaxxers are suffering from that so-called CoVax Syndrome (lethargy, severe weakness and fatigue, symptoms resembling stress or burnout, severe shooting pain, problems with seeing and hearing, depression).

Among adolescents and young adults, Covid injections have already caused 250 times more deaths than the (presumed) coronavirus (3). Adams therefore finds it incomprehensible that these 'vaccines' can still be called 'safe and effective'. 'These are crimes against humanity under the pretext of vaccinations.' He even warns of 'an upcoming vaccine holocaust.'

Chapter 17: Climate hoax and Future Dictatorship 2030?

Greenland just experienced record increase in ice - Brazil loses 10 million bags of coffee due to COLD - The harsh reality of global cooling will eventually pulverize the CO2 global warming fairy tale

Climate lockdowns will become permanent, as according to UN Agenda-21 / 2030, all people must be locked up in megacities, and they will be banned from free access to nature.

Worldwide, thousands of real scientists have not taken the IPCC - the UN climate panel run by far-left ideologues and 'experts' approved by them - seriously for years. How different is it with politicians and mainstream media, who either out of conviction or gullible ignorance have fully embraced this demagogic fake science agenda, which has only one goal: to totally demolish freedom, democracy and prosperity in the West, and subject the whole world to a totalitarian communist dictatorship. The latest IPCC 'doomsday' report is again full of demonstrable nonsense about global warming, and is only intended to scare the population even more and make them ripe for permanent 'climate' lockdowns.

UN Secretary-General Guterres already announced the 'climate emergency' late last year, which is to be maintained until 'climate neutrality' is achieved in 2050.

This means that for the next 30 years or so we will be plunged into climate lockdowns, which will follow each other in such quick succession that soon there will be a permanent situation that will never be reversed even after 2050.

The goal: total control over everything and everyone

The goal of the globalist UN/WHO/WEF/EU/IMF elite is well known to you all by now: total control over everything and everyone - literally. The IPCC is now trying to give a reason in advance for the coming food, fuel and energy shortages, and the spreading chaos and poverty that will result, with the lie of "accelerated man-made warming". The real cause of climate change, a continuing cooling due to the new Grand Solar Minimum and the rapidly weakening magnetic field of the earth, will probably never be admitted.

You cannot control the sun, and you cannot tax our star either, so the climate alarmists in politics, media and institutions such as IPCC will continue with their fake science panic messages demanding that human CO2 emissions must go to zero to stop a climate catastrophe, and that you and I must make great sacrifices that will lead to the irrevocable end of our freedom and current prosperity, and with it things like affordable energy and food, reliable heating and private transport.

Sun and climate don't care about Western dictate

Meanwhile, the sun and the climate do not care about the false CO2 dictate of the Western alarmists. Due to severe cold in South America, Argentina and Brazil now have to import large quantities of food. In Brazil, 10 million bags of coffee have already been lost due to persistent COLD. In South Africa, too, crops have been badly hit by record cold. In the US, cold and drought threaten to reduce grain harvests by as much as 70% (what will Americans have to eat soon?), and images of flood disasters in Europe and China went around the world.

'Climate change' has always been there and will always be there. The mild, perfectly normal warming of the last century was a much-needed recovery from the Dalton Minimum, a cold period of crop failure, disease, shortages and poverty.

It is not humans, but global cooling that historically always causes unstable and more extreme weather conditions. The alarmists in politics and media are only spreading the dogmatic, anti-scientific fairy tale that the climate is always supposed to remain nearly constant and stable, and something like a few fractions of a percent extra CO2 would cause catastrophic warming.

Unfortunately, our future is cold

Rising temperatures = more stable weather, good harvests, fewer diseases, better living conditions, and greater biodiversity. This has always been true since time immemorial. That's why tropical forests contain the majority of all species of plants and animals on Earth, despite occupying only 12% of the land surface. That's why civilizations flourished during periods of rising temperatures, and fell into decline again when it got colder.

Falling temperatures = ALWAYS big problems. Life has much more difficulty adapting to cold than to heat. Look at the poles; only 600 species of plants live there, 100 species of birds, no reptiles and amphibians, and only 20 species of mammals. Cold = unstable weather = poor and failed harvests = hunger = diseases = shortages = war, and lots of misery and death.

Unfortunately our future is cold, and unfortunately that future has already begun. The sun has entered a new Grand Solar Minimum, a 400 year cycle that will cause prolonged cooling with sharply lower temperatures. The IPCC does not want you to know this. In fact, the IPCC refuses to even consider this, because otherwise these facts undercut their AGW (Anthropogenic Global Warming) fantasy. Also the government does not want you to know this, and is breaking down the very thing that could help us get through this cold period: stable, affordable energy (oil, gas, nuclear, coal), and is swapping it for extremely weather-dependent, unsustainable and very expensive 'green' sources.

Influence of the sun is just maximal

105

The IPCC claims that the sun's influence on climate is minimal. This is simplistic, not to say downright ridiculous, because in addition to the hard facts from history, real scientists show time and again that the sun is the single biggest driver of climate change. For example, a weaker sun allows more cosmic rays to enter our atmosphere, increasing volcanic activity and promoting cloud formation, things that greatly affect temperature.

A recent astronomical study found that the far too high temperature on Jupiter - a mystery that could not be explained in 50 years - is caused by the intense aurora (= solar activity) around the planet, which has a powerful impact on the magnetic field. This decisive effect of cosmic rays on the atmospheres of planets, and thus the weather and temperature, is completely ignored by the IPCC. The same applies to the amplifying effect resulting from our planet's rapidly diminishing magnetic field.

The UN climate panel, despite numerous scientific studies, has simply decided that the sun should have no influence on the climate, because this completely undermines their CO2 theory and thus their right to exist. This is pure ideologically driven quackery, which in history only knows its equal in the 'scientists' that the Vatican drummed up to 'prove' that the Earth was the center of the universe, and was really flat and not round.

Extremely LOW level of CO2 in atmosphere

In addition, simple undeniable facts, such as the mere 450 parts per million of CO2 in our atmosphere (= 0.04%) which is historically an extremely LOW level* (but just above the limit at which life is possible on Earth (300 ppm)), should make even the least thoughtful, most docile people without any scientific knowledge wonder why such a fuss is made about a minute increase of a perfectly natural and necessary gas for all life, which is criminally misrepresented as a 'poisonous gas'.

(* On a geological time scale, there was once 7000 ppm CO2 in the atmosphere. The planet was NOT covered in water then because all the ice would have melted from the heat).

But unfortunately 99 out of 100 people have an innate slave mentality. If someone with enough power and authority claims something, they will automatically believe it, no matter how much evidence there is to the contrary, no matter how diametric and obtuse the message and policy. Inept docility seems to be in all of us DNA, and the psychopathic power mongers who always and everywhere manage to make it to the top are all too happy to abuse it historically.

Fake 'warming' models that have nothing to do with reality

Fake 'warming' models that have nothing to do with reality

And so you get fake models based on which trillions of euros and dollars are taken from society (healthcare, education, work, quality of life, development) to fund climate policies, despite the fact that none of those models have come even close to reality. Do you remember the IPCC's earlier nonsense? The North Pole was supposed to have melted completely first by 2000, then by 2012, and then by 2020, snow was supposed to be a thing of the past, and entire coastal areas were supposed to have been flooded with water (Florida, Europe, etc.). It all turned out to be your purest bullshit.

CODE RED because of power grab climate-vaccine cult

But the thousands of scientists who have a totally different view from the IPCC based on the hard facts are not heard and do not get into the media. Instead, the public is constantly inundated with alarmist fake news reports and blaring headlines like "Code Red for Humanity. There is only one reason for this, and it is not called the climate, but totalitarian control over ALL aspects of your life through the implementation of disruptive 'climate lockdowns', ostensibly to 'save the planet and humanity', but in reality to condemn you to a poor and miserable slave existence from which there is no escape.

Climate and Covid/vaccine policies are causing disastrous and irreparable damage to the global food supply, transportation chains, economy and quality of life. During the coming "climate lockdowns," the population will be much easier to control once it finally rebels due to ongoing food and energy shortages, and even more draconian measures can be quickly imposed. You will no longer have any say or freedom, and a large part of your wealth will have disappeared (see also our article of 12-01: Deutsche Bank: Green Deal EU means mega crisis, eco-dictatorship and great loss of wealth).

So there is indeed CODE RED for humanity. However, not because of the climate, but because of the by almost all parties supported climate-vaccine sect that has taken our complete political system in a stranglehold, and that wants to subject our people, the world and the future in a rapid tempo to a communist UN/WHO/WEF/EU/IMF world authority, the hardest, most inhumane dictatorship this planet has ever known.

Our other books

Check out our other books for other unreported news, exposed facts and debunked truths, and more.

Join the exclusive Rebel Press Media Circle!

You will get new updates about the unreported reality delivered in your inbox every Friday.

Sign up here today:

https://campsite.bio/rebelpressmedia